SPELLCRAFT: A PRIMER

SPELLCRAFT: A PRIMER

EL MORNINGSTAR

PREFACE

You don't know the author, and it's for the best.

The author is not interested in collegiality, and makes no pretense to be the best or only practitioner. The author's aim with this work is simple and selfish. The more practitioners there are, the more camouflaged (and therefore safer) the author is.

Besides, the author may or may not be paying off a bargain or two by publishing. You never know.

Herein lies the first lesson: **Consider the source, take what is useful and leave what isn't.** Different techniques unlock the gates for different practitioners. Experimentation and common sense are key in magick as well as in more prosaic pursuits. *Know thyself* isn't just good mental hygiene, it's also a strategy for deciphering what transgressions or acts hold enough power to be useful.

Herein lies the second lesson: **Do the work, then decide.** With practice comes discrimination. Any new skill—and magick is a highly skilled endeavor—requires enough time and effort spent to acquire familiarity. Mistakes will teach you as much as success.

Herein lies the last lesson: **Be careful what you wish for, lest it happen.** The most common cause of failure is the refusal to prepare the physical ground so your spell dies shortly after germination. The second most common is deep fear of success. Spells tend to serve up what we really want, not what we *think* we want, and such an operation is terrifying for those who do not practice the requisite self-honesty.

I shall assume most readers have enough familiarity with correspondences, sympathetic magick, tarot, and pop culture to understand certain references. For those who do not, practicing basic research skills will do no harm. The scope of this work does not afford digression into certain fascinating areas and likewise precludes much academic nicety.

⬟

Now, let us begin.

PART I

THEORY

REASONS

Magick requires effort, especially spells, so why bother?

There are three main reasons given for pursuing the Art; most common is for personal fulfilment or advancement. There is absolutely nothing wrong with this. Ambition and achievement are no more liable to toxicity than any other human drive. Western culture's view of both as inherently evil is both a function of repression and the fear of those mediocre enough to accept the status quo. Ambition can be selfish or selfless; striving for achievement prompts humanity to rise or even just roll out of bed.

The second most common reason is revenge. If you're seeking vengeance against the less powerful, you're a tyrant; while you might garner some initial success, the consequences are highly and increasingly unpleasant. Vengeance against those more powerful is far more attractive—and far less prone to severe ill effects. Spite is good fuel and an excellent motivator, as long as it's directed well.

The last in the trifecta of most common reasons is liberation itself, whether from political or other oppression. Those who turn up their noses at the Art are often those with the least to lose under the status quo and the most to gain from disrupting oppression. Magick, especially witchcraft, is a way of evening the odds and can be used to decolonize and to heal. This motivation, like spite, is excellent; its drawbacks include fanaticism—always a detriment when practicing—and burnout.

Just because these are the most common reasons doesn't mean they're the only ones, or that any combination of reasons is morally superior or mutually exclusive. Other reasons may include:

⬠

- *Because it looks cool.* Pop culture fascination with the hidden and the occult draws many to the practice. Movies and fiction serve as an entry point for many, and serve to create a "grammar" of the invisible world that can be harnessed by the adept practitioner. They also provide protective camouflage for the serious. The time of violence against those who tread the pathways of the occult is not yet past. It may never be past; safety is a prime consideration for any serious practitioner.
- *Because it's there.* Some are simply curious, stealing fire for a lark. Human beings are inveterate rock-turners and curtain-pullers.
- *Desperation.* When one has tried everything else, there's little to lose by engaging in magick. Often, that very

desperation provides some necessary preconditions for success, like full concentration of all one's psychic and physical resources upon a matter or the willingness to look ridiculous in order to be effective.

- *Sex*. The attraction of the hidden or trappings of the occult have often been used to find willing partners or attempt to pressure unwilling ones. As with spite, this is a powerful motivator as long as it's directed well and engages *only the willing*. Pressuring an unwilling partner of any gender is rape, and has hideous consequences—including impotence and severe injury—for the perpetrator.

⬡

Any combination of reasons will do to fuel one's practice, as long as one's willing to put the effort of actual practice in. Nobody else is entitled to know or care what yours are, but *you* should. Knowing why one wishes to achieve a particular goal is useful for planning and preparation as well as mitigating any possible side effects. The only reason to care *why* one wishes to be a practitioner, whether witch, sorcerer, or whatever other name, is in order to point to the most efficient way of achieving one's goal.

Any reason for any action can be selfish or noble, it's all in the application—like magick itself.

RISKS AND EFFECTS

Magick is, in essence, a set of techniques. Serious application of any technique, no matter the desired end, has common risks and effects.

By far the most common effect of the regular and serious practice of magick is the strengthening of certain sensitivities. The mental and psychic muscles respond to exercise much like their physical counterparts; it's common for inexplicable or extrasensory phenomena to spike at the beginning of magickal practice, plateau, and spike again as long as consistent effort is applied. The most dangerous time for many practitioners is during the plateau period, when results may seem small compared to the effort expended and the temptation to cease proper, regular work is at its highest.

The next most common effect, quite logically, is isolation. Not only do several branches of occult practice and many spells enjoin silence upon the practitioner, but the risk of being singled out for opprobrium, censure, ridicule, or physical threat induces many to keep their studies and experiments quiet. With the advent of modern communication technology, the loneliness and need for extreme secrecy is easing somewhat—a blessing for some and an irritant to others, indeed. The ease with which a practitioner may anonymously correspond with other serious students of the occult has been a great boon to study and experimentation.

Another extremely common effect is strange coincidence. The world, both visible and otherwise, tends to arrange itself in certain patterns around the serious practitioner; those not ready for a cascade of weirdness tend to drop away from the work as soon as real results begin to appear. Those with a higher tolerance and a healthy sense of the absurd self-select into higher practice, as in many other creative or psychically draining endeavors.

Less interesting, and far more dangerous, is the risk of paranoia. Caution is healthy; a practitioner understands the need for self-defense. However, seeing enemies visible and invisible behind every rock and tree is hardly a reasonable way to live, and fritters away necessary energy as well as control. Likewise, arrogance, while useful and motivating in small measures, can easily metastasize into a liability.

Another significant but often overstated risk is attention from invisible or non-human sources. Whether these sources are deep psychological events/currents or actual non-corporeal entities is entirely academic; what is *not* academic are the risks of coming to their notice. The emphasis upon protection and cleansing in many magickal traditions not only serves as a ritual trigger for certain modes of consciousness but also provides strong bulwarks against psychosis *and* predation.

Many practitioners, whether of witchcraft, sorcery, or any other branch, fall into the trap of thinking appurtenances and pedantry are a substitute for regular, consistent magickal work. Accessories and texts, especially the more expensive ones, can be very satisfying and useful, but they are nothing compared to actual, practical experience. Always aim for the latter.

Lastly, though isolation is a risk, visibility and exposure can be just as dangerous or detrimental. While some traditions are woven into a cultural fabric that gives them deep significance and protection, or may even provide practitioners with a robust framework of mutually beneficial teachers and disciples, this is by no means the rule. The reactions of non-practitioners can range from mild amusement to fanatical attack, not to mention the significant percentage of those who would take advantage of your hard work without properly compensating you—*if* you let them. Each practitioner must balance the risks of isolation and visibility in their own way. The practitioners who choose to practice visibly, or to perform works of mass consciousness-raising, must be cognizant of the risks if they intend to survive.

PART II

SOME BASICS

TERMS

Many, bastardizing a Crowley quote, call magick *the art of changing consciousness at will*. A practitioner will add, *in order to achieve an effect*. The effect may be the change in consciousness itself or a tangible event, according to circumstances. In Western occult culture, there are two main ways to go about achieving such effects, sorcery and witchcraft.

Sorcery is the art of enforcing your will on the world, while *witchcraft* works with natural forces to achieve one's ends. The terms are used largely for convenience. Both are magick, and there are borderlands where the two blur into each other. By and large, while most witches are fair sorcerers when the occasion calls for it, sorcerers tend to be extremely ineffective witches.

Sorcery is magick by fiat; a sorcerer is often a practitioner who begins without innate psychic ability or with such ability blocked for whatever psychological reason. Since they cannot see or sense the energies involved, they tend to be literalists and ceremonialists, seeking aged texts or "traditions" to provide crucial confidence in the initial stages. Any regular, disciplined magickal practice tends to strengthen and awaken psychic or extrasensory abilities, so sorcerers tend to become more sensitive over time, though their habits may ossify somewhat. The hardening is both a blessing and a risk, since it paves the way for quick, reflexive magickal acts in one sense but also closes off many avenues of exploration and play that might make one's practice more effective.

Witchcraft, on the other hand, tends to collect those with some innate sensitivity; they display a marked preference for "catching" a tide of natural energy and riding it much as a surfer does. The initial sensitivity sometimes means they don't see the need for commitment and steady practice; the tendency of dilettantism in witches is rather marked. While this boradens the range of tools witches have available in any situation, it also robs many tools of their full utility by the lack of diligent practice.

Both methods have much to recommend them. Sorcery can most often aid in accumulating markers of outward success, or in harnessing non-human or incorporeal beings to work the practitioner's will. Witchcraft tends to much stronger protections—practitioners often are said to "sink" into the ambient atmosphere and be very difficult to attack—and aid in psychic or physical healing, as well as harnessing natural tides and forces to add strength and depth to their spells.

It's helpful to view these definitions and distinctions as making a continuum rather than two separate species. Most Western practitioners are hybrid with definite preferences, rather than strictly one or the other. Modern technology means practitioners can sample a wide range of techniques, including those from other cultures, which has a tremendous democratizing effect but also leads to the paralysis of choice and issues of appropriation. Divisions in other cultural occult frameworks are beyond the scope of this little book.

In the end, it matters little what end of the spectrum a practitioner leans towards. What matters, only and always, is *results*.

RESEARCH

Research is as essential as experimentation, and literacy is key to many magickal traditions and systems. To that end, whether witch or sorcerer, the practitioner must read widely. In the beginning, discriminating between useful and useless texts is rather a handicap; it's better to be voracious when starting out to accumulate a wide view than to lose precious time and energy sinking into a tradition or author who may or may not give one results. Later, even the most useless or trite occult or semi-occult books may provide simple amusement or a single germ of truth buried in its dredge, but one cannot tell dross from gold without benchmarks attained from wide reading and experimentation.

Many practitioners make the mistake of reading *only* occult or New-Age-flavored books. History, philosophy, science, and other nonfiction is also essential. The more one understands of how the world works, the more tolerant and inquisitive one is of other areas of human experience or scientific knowledge, the more effective a practitioner becomes and the more robust their methods. A certain historical vignette may expand one's understanding of a traditional magical form, or a scientific theory or effect give one ideas on the handling of energy and subtle forces.

Fiction in its many forms should not be neglected, either. Imagination, the refusal to accept things as they are, and the empathy required to understand characters have obvious advantages in systematic, personal magickal practice. In order to change, first one must be able to imagine something different.

The discipline of reading and the effort of becoming an autodidact is wonderful practice for solo magickal work. Though reading is the most common way to absorb magickal and other information, those with learning or other disabilities need not despair; it is the study that counts, in whatever way you are able to perform it. Accessibility is by no means currently perfect, though much better than it was before computers and cloud-based anonymity. Should one choose to share one's knowledge, it's always best to provide what accessibility you can to serious students of any ability.

MAGICKAL OBJECTS

Humans are physical creatures, with a unique capacity to affect the physical world. While it's possible to bring about change with sheer simple stubborn willpower, it's easier and more effective in almost any case to find a physical object to "charge" with magickal force in order to enact one's desires.

"Magickal object" is a catchall term for physical objects charged with magical energy for specific purposes. This includes poppets, witch bottles, athames, grimoires, ceremonial objects and jewelry, wands—anything with a specific purpose and a physical matrix for holding an energy charge. Whether that energy is purely psychological and the object meant to trigger alternative consciousness or a subtle, discrete power currently unable to be scientifically measured is, again, academic. What matters is that physical objects work in a variety of ways for the practitioner.

Some schools of study, mainly ceremonial and sorcerous, draw a heavy, clear distinction between magickal objects and "profane" daily implements. Others, mainly hedge- and kitchen-witchery, are of the opinion that any tool used with intent becomes magickal by default for as long as that intent remains. Some will argue that the former allows for a greater magickal charge, but it's a matter of personal preference as well as finance. Without the discipline of practice and commitment, any magickal object is merely a toy, and in times of need an experienced practitioner can make anything serve as a talisman, magickal weapon, or magickal aid. As the saying goes, any stick may become a wand.

The term "sigil" used to mean a geometric figure functioning as a name and a calling method for angels—or demons, or sheer elemental or astrological forces. In current magickal theory, however, the meaning encompasses not only the previous sense but also a method of condensing a goal into a simplified, abstract shape, which is inscribed on a material—paper, wood, clay, etc.—and charged with force to work the practitioner's will. Sigils are powerful, unobtrusive, and can be retained as amulets or forgotten immediately after release, which makes them ideal for a wide range of problems and projects; they are often classified as magickal objects as they are marked into a physical matrix in order to be charged.

While the patina on an antique, pre-owned, or expensive object can be comforting, it's often best to make do with the simplest objects using materials you can buy, make, or obtain with a minimum of trouble. On the other hand, very little matches the thrill of finding a perfect ceremonial or magickal item at the right moment and carrying one's prize home.

Some practitioners go out of their way to acquire antique magickal objects from cultures not their own, as a shortcut to accumulating power.

The practice might be marginally excusable if it was indeed a shortcut or had a solid record of working, but it has neither and all too often is simply acquisitiveness or outright theft masquerading as an interest in the occult. Such items and practitioners are to be viewed with deep suspicion and outright derision.

BARGAINS

Magickal systems and practices are as varied and as old as humanity itself, but every single one contains the notion of—and instructions for the practice of—bargains with nonhuman or inhuman influences. Should one not find evidence of such things in one's chosen system, deeper and more intensive research will inevitably turn it up.

From soliciting the protection of a loa or a Holy Guardian Angel to binding a familiar spirit, from a pact with a demon or prayer to an deity, from an agreement to an oricha to an agreement with local fairies, from the bond of shaman and totem to animal familiars, bargains are a deep intrinsic part of magickal practice. Bartering with whoever or whatever has the power to protect or provide is an old, cooperative human instinct.

It makes little difference whether the practitioner is using the mythology of bargains to harness deep psychological forces or to sign a contract with a sentient incorporeal entity. There are naysayers who will call it a desperate need for any control in the face of humanity's random, utter cosmic insignificance, too. The only measure a practitioner should apply is, does it work, and if it doesn't, are there compelling enough reasons to try again?

This is entirely separate from the safety considerations, which are largely self-evident. Every contract presupposes recourse if the terms are broken and also provides a measure of protection. Research to determine the traditional forms such contracts take will provide the sagacious practitioner with invaluable insight as well as an idea of how to modify terms for one's best benefit.

PART III

CAUTION AND INCAUTION

COMMON SENSE

The latter part of this work will be an examination of the basic structure of spells, which are a subset of magickal acts, and will touch only briefly on basic divination—a whole subject in and of itself, which must be left to a later work. First, however, a few words of caution.

REHEARSE, REHEARSE, REHEARSE

By far the best ally in any magickal practice is common sense—a skill like any other, but regrettably *un*common through the ages.

Candles, costumes, chanting, and incense are all very nice, but one's house/clothing/hair catching fire, or a translated recipe for incense that produces a poisonous fume, are not mere nuisances but deadly dangers. Extreme care must be taken in mixing or preparing homemade oils, unguents, perfumes, and especially incense, which is readily available and relatively cheap. When in doubt, use the simplest and safest option available until one has acquired the necessary information and expertise to attempt more complex recipes.

Ritual clothing should be comfortable instead of aesthetic. It's difficult to achieve the requisite concentration, let alone relaxation, in a binding, pinching, flame-welcoming garment, no matter *how* fashionable. Those who practice skyclad should take care to have proper protection for feet or any tender anatomical areas, and hair should be dressed simply and securely in order to avoid incident.

Some practitioners enjoy the challenge of complex ritual and feel they are more powerful; others aim for minimalism in everything; still others hold that a complex non-effort comparable to Zen is the goal. One's personal preferences are powerful guides, but are *only* tour guides; striking off the path is not only the prerogative but the duty of the practitioner. Practice and rehearsal will help rituals go smoothly, especially when just starting out, and will alert one to possible hazards.

As in warfare, no plan in ritual or spellwork survives contact with actual ground conditions. However, planning and rehearsal are indispensable to gain trust and confidence in one's own abilities and open up vistas for improvisation. Rehearsals and practice can also accumulate a slight but significantly useful magickal charge, which will only deepen results. Practice is your friend, and will allow you to react quickly when the unexpected strikes.

The most likely problem, however, is a very human desire to use a new tool for everything but what it was designed and acquired for. Magick will not stop a bully's punch—but it may help one avoid the bully's notice, indirectly arrange a situation where the bully is sent elsewhere or given consequences, or give one confidence and inner resources to endure and thrive.

A hammer is a hammer, a drill press is a drill press, magick…is magick, and should not be used as a hammer, a drill press, or a washcloth.

THE TERROR OF RESULTS

By far the most insidious, invidious danger to the occult practitioner is the absolute terror of real results. The single most common response to a genuine paranormal, magickal, or extraordinary occurrence in the vast majority of the population is to run the other direction as quickly as possible. Many otherwise promising students retreat into empty formalism or aggressive, pathological skepticism the first time they touch the live wire of *actual change* or super-weirdness they thought they wanted.

This is not an act of cowardice—the case could be made that it is an act of profound, rational sense. Nor is continuing after such an encouraging result a sign of foolhardiness. The choice is simply there to be made, and can always be revisited.

Those who gain a real result and retreat into formalism or skepticism are not to be pitied or condescended to. They have simply made a choice with their own personal practice. It's all too human to feel a fond amusement or irritation at formalists or pedants, but as long as they harm no-one, no response or investment is required from the continuing practitioner.

Practitioners should be cautious of this effect in other ways, too. While it might be amusing or satisfy a deep inner need to unnerve others with effects or performances, any breath of genuine extraordinariness will inevitably call a cascade of fear onto the practitioner's head. And what human beings fear, they tend to strike out at. Even the best of intentions and the most innocuous of spells can quickly become evidence of strangeness to be eradicated without mercy.

Those who wish to harness the power of crowds or practitioners whose vanity is tickled by leading public rituals would do well to reconsider. Today's magickal hero is the tomorrow's sacrificed scapegoat. Still, it is your choice. Choose wisely what to do with your own fear of results, and never forget the danger of others'.

NO CHOSEN ONES

The astute reader will have noticed the emphasis on personal choice and preference. The practice of the Art is not forced upon unwilling victims. Anyone born with extraordinary sensitivities can choose to let them atrophy, anyone born with little can use diligent practice to sharpen what they have. Aptitude does not mean willingness or desire, while practice and discipline build aptitude—no matter how incrementally.

There are no chosen ones. In magick, the practitioner chooses.

THE RULE OF THREE

There is a popular canard in current occultism, the famous "Rule of Three" or "Threefold Law." On the surface, it seems simple: *Whatever the occultist sends into the world will return threefold, good for good, evil for evil.*

An invention of Gerald Gardiner, no doubt the Threefold Law is supposed to mean "consequences" or "karma," both heavily misused concepts in their own right. More often, and more prosaically, the Law used to shame or browbeat several schools of practitioners wholesale, or as a cover for passive-aggressive behavior. The real question is "who is defining evil, and do they benefit by doing so?"

There are other questions to be considered as well. Who is more ethical, the practitioner who refrains from destructive or offensive magick from fear of punishment, or the practitioner who refrains though they will not be "punished" in any way? If the Threefold Law is a bedrock magickal law, as it is touted to be, why do its effects not bring about a more equitable state in the physical realm? Who decides what is good and what is evil, from which vantage point? Whose morals override another's?

Multiplying good things for one's friends or tribe—not to mention bad things for enemies or a rival tribe—is endemic in magickal history, not to mention human nature. Erasing or suppressing that half—or more than half—of natural human behavior features in much dystopic literature and even more totalitarianisms, and the effect is to make the ignored, viciously repressed tendencies more savage and bloodthirsty, prone to leaping free whenever the superego is distracted.

Furthermore, if one is reduced to the level of a creeping supplicant, only "thinking good thoughts" for fear of anything that might rebound badly, why would one ever wish to do magick at all?

Another "law" often mentioned is Crowley's *do as thou wilt*, which in the original context was hedged with a few significant qualifications. There is the matter of the laws of sympathetic magick, as well.

Magick, especially when used as a process of self-discovery, requires the practitioner to interrogate their own ethics before action as a matter of course. A practitioner who does not risks unpleasant side-effects indeed. More than that, it is the duty and measure of a responsible human being to think deeply on such questions not just once but consistently and nigh constantly.

How much more so, then, for a sorcerer or a witch who truly believes in their abilities—or even simply wants to believe in order to strengthen them?

PART IV

PRACTICE

MAGICKAL ACT

Magickal acts are a diverse group, which vary from culture to culture. Knocking on wood for luck, blessing someone who sneezes, wishing on birthday candles, tossing salt over the shoulder, avoiding cracks that "break a parent's back," tossing flowers at weddings, breaking a fortune cookie, burning paper twists to carry a request, wearing a saint's medal—all these and more qualify in their own ways as magickal acts. Most play upon custom, tradition, forgotten religious observance, or sympathetic magick and correspondences and are performed somewhat habitually, if seldom neglected.

Not all magickal acts are spells, but all spells are magical acts. Spells follow a basic structure, almost always centered a physical item or framework to hold a magickal charge:

- Preparation
- Building

- Charging
- Release
- Silence

What is important is the buildup of energy followed by the concentration and the willpower to direct that energy into the prepared object or framework. Some aspects of the structure can be whole spells of their own, especially the ritual cleansings often used in the preparation phase. Using a charged item is a magickal act but not necessarily a spell; what makes a spell is the structure itself.

As with any definition, there are grey areas. The recitation in many Western ceremonial magick systems, or the chanting of sutras in others, could be considered spells in and of themselves since each time the chant or sutra is used it accretes power from both the practitioner and the practitioner's cultural background—the argument against considering them so hinges on them being more in the nature of spoken talismans adhered to reflexively, with little intent. Still others advance the notion that the act of recitation may serve a double function in alerting intelligences one is beseeching for protection that their aid is required and in lulling the practitioner's mind into a variety of ritual consciousness. It is very likely a combination, depending on circumstances.

Other grey areas include some who insist sigils must be either spells or magickal objects, not both, and the vexing question of shamanic flight and the exact nexus of culture and magickal energy. However fascinating, this is not the place to indulge.

Charms are structured similarly to spells, but without the charging and release of significant energy. One may commit a magickal act instinctively or reflexively, or even perform a charm on the fly, but a spell requires preparation.

PART V

THE TRIO

CLEANSING, PROTECTION, DIVINATION

For the purposes of this work, it is assumed that the practitioner has already decided the effect they intend to achieve—the *purpose* of the spell—and has decided upon a basic method for achieving it—the *form* of the spell. With those decided, it becomes a question of actual performance, which begins with the the trinity of cleansing, protection, and divination.

Cleansing is not meant to imply that regular life is somehow dirty or polluted, as some dualists would have it. Instead, it prepares the mind and body to enter ritual space—much as an athlete's or musician's habitual pre-game or pre-concert psych-ups prepare for performace—and makes sure no influences but the ones the practitioner wants affect the work.

It is also a necessary step in deciding parameters. The most intense spellwork can be frittered away by improper aim, or have unpleasant, unintended effects because of improper framing. The cleansing, protection, and divination aspects of basic initial spellwork are meant to concentrate force and cut down on unintended effects. A spell is power unleashed; once completed, you can no more stop effects than you can return the water from a burst dam.

Cleansing can include washing or ablution of the physical body and arrangement of the ritual space, censing with incense or other fumes, sprinkling water or perfume, chanting or ritual movements with an appropriate implement, sweeping with a besom, or even good old-fashioned physical dusting, vacuuming, mopping, and arranging.

Like cleansing, protection doesn't imply or require an inimical or dirty world. Though ritual consciousness is vulnerable in many ways, it is no more so than regular waking consciousness. There is more chance of vital energy being bled away by improper containment than of an invisible predator or some form of "contagion" entering your ritual space. On the other hand, the feeling of safety frees up a great deal of the practitioner's mental and psychic energy, and there is no reason *not* to have the insurance of protective methods that have been used by practitioners throughout the history of the Art.

Protection can include casting a circle—a seventeenth-century invention that has proved quite useful—or invoking one's particular deities or guardian angels. There are as many methods as there are practitioners, and a physical tool can be used to great effect when setting magickal protections in place. A witch's athame can delineate ritual space, focus energy, and provide cleansing; a besom or a sorcerer's wand may do the same. Protection is most likely to involve some physical items, both for ease and for the practitioner's comfort.

The trio's last sister, divination by whatever method, is meant more to alert the practitioner to possible mental blocks and pitfalls than to ward off celestial interference or serve up a movie-worthy mental montage, though such things are not un-heard-of.

Divination deserves an entire book of its own; suffice to say whatever method a practitioner uses is merely a blank screen for whatever precognitive talent is available to project upon and in the process, strengthen itself. Many prospective practitioners accumulate the pretty appurtenances of various divination methods without working with one consistently to strengthen precognitive ability, and while collection is pleasant it should not be mistaken for actual work.

Repeated cleansing, protection work, and divination also help accrue magickal force and ease the triggering of ritual consciousness, much as repeated regular workouts strengthen the physical body. Some practitioners cleanse before every divination, others regularly refresh standard protections on their homes or places of ritual work in order to increase the efficacy both of its intended purposes and triggering ritual consciousness. Regular protection work is most recommended for any practitioner worth the name.

Divination and protection also serve the purpose of sharpening the practitioner's "magickal grammar"—the confluence of practice, prop, and psychological oddity that triggers the requisite changes in the psyche. What works for one practitioner may not—indeed, often flat-out *will* not—for another. The process of self-discovery necessary to find the magickal acts that resonate most with one's particular mental and physical individuality is shifted into high gear with regular practice, especially of divination.

Once the spell's intended effects are decided upon, divination has shown the way around blocks and pitfalls, the ritual space is clear and prepared, and the practitioner has arrived at the point of actual casting, it becomes necessary to raise a magickal charge in order to fuel the desired change.

PART VI

BUILDING, CHARGING

ABNEGATION, SEX, SACRIFICE

There are several ways to raise magickal energy for the purpose of spell-release. The most common are abnegation, sex, and sacrifice.

Planned, conscious self-denial creates a great deal of tension that can be harnessed for magick. The most common method is to deny oneself certain foods, much in the manner of religious dietary prohibitions. The denial of certain other stimulants or depressants—such as tobacco, alcohol, caffeine—can provide a powerful if somewhat transient charge as well. Care must be taken that the abnegation is *conscious*, *deliberate*, and *non-ordinary*. Refraining from a certain food because of allergy or distaste is, alas, not quite enough. Refraining from certain condiments or spices has also been advocated, but this often provides only trivial effects.

Some practitioners begin their self-denial during the initial cleansing phase. Others advocate various periods of outright fasting to serve the multiple purposes of cleansing, triggering certain physical changes facilitating magickal consciousness, and gathering power. The benefits of fasting are attested to by its appearance not only in magickal literature but in widespread religious traditions; the dangers are self-apparent and should be carefully considered before any attempt.

A medical practitioner should be consulted to make sure the physical body will not suffer undue or health-threatening strain with short-term fasting, and physical medical issues should be taken into account. Humanity's great asset is our physicality; it should not be squandered, and a healthy physical body makes the demands of magickal practice that much lighter.

Once one has decided on abnegation as your method, some experimentation is needed to find the methods of self-denial that will provide the most necessary, greatest, safest, or quickest charge according to the practitioner's needs. Remember, magick is a *practice*.

Another very commonly performed method of raising power is sexual continence. While initially useful, especially during cleansing, such asceticism tends to become farcical in later stages. A period of repression makes the eventual release that much more powerful, but as with all spectacular fuel, the amount necessary to propel without shredding the container is finely calibrated.

It is also common practice (though rarely spoken of directly) to dedicate a sexual act with a willing partner to a particular spell, though special care must be taken to secure enthusiastic consent at every stage. Far more common is raising power through masturbation. In such cases, not only is the energy harnessed by concentration upon the desired end at the moment of climax, but a small amount of fluid(s) from the encounter upon the spell's physical matrix creates a powerful, ongoing sympathetic link.

The last common spell fuel is sacrifice, a word which has so many religious and other overtones a word or three of explanation is required. Animal sacrifice has featured in religions worldwide, and much ceremonial magick took its cues from the religious engineers of ritual space. It is perfectly possible for the act of intentionally killing another creature to raise a magickal charge, and perfectly possible for that charge to be caught and channeled into a spell. **It is categorically not necessary *or* ethically defensible unless one's culture currently practices such acts.** Non-subsistence hunting is also not a recommended fuel for spellwork, for obvious reasons.

Lesser sacrifices—in the religious sense—of such things as perfumes, ungents, items of clothing, first fruits, are also not what is implied in the magickal term.

A distinction must also be made between a more intense form of religious self-abnegation, commonly called self-sacrifice, and sacrifice in a magickal sense. The former is supplicatory, not even bargaining since the other party cannot be held to terms. The latter is an action akin to pressing an accelerator to feed more fuel to an engine.

On the other hand, the intentional shedding of one's own blood (with properly prepared tools and appropriate wound care) is a powerful act, reserved for the deepest and most important works. There are also practitioners who find slight, occasional self-inflicted pain more reliable or appropriate for their magickal ends, though extreme care must be taken with anything approaching that method. Sacrifice is magickal, self-harm is not.

There are a few other methods of raising force

for a spell, including (but not limited to) ritual dance, chant, and communal festivities. Of these, the most interesting is the capture of the force of the spontaneous eruption of a crowd's feeling during a concert, sporting, or similar event. The essential component is the rising tension and the desired end held firmly in mind at the point of climax.

The astute reader will already have noticed that in certain cases, these methods may blur into each other. A practitioner may find a combination of fuels particularly effective for certain spells. Of critical importance is not to become too dependent on any one fuel or process in particular. Flexibility keeps a practitioner adapting and effective far longer than slavish devotion to habit or dogma.

Said reader will also have noticed no mention has been made so far of sacred or magickal inebriation. Psychoactive compounds are useful in shamanism and specialized branches of magick, the former as a matter of course in the related culture and the latter under strict, quasi-laboratory conditions. Shamanism lies outside the scope of this small work; the ersatz, culturally appropriative hedonist's gulping of questionable substances for ill-defined ends is beneath it. A well-practiced and disciplined sorcerer may enter trance or alternative consciousness in short while, a practicing witch within a few breaths, and in both cases no ingestion of any substance is required.

There remain practitioners determined to use stimulants or depressants as fuel, and the monotony of their fates is almost superseded by its banality.

PART VII

RELEASE

CUTTING THE CORD

The release of power that fuels a spell lasts a few moments. What follows? The most tongue-in-cheek answer is, "Cleanup."

Some practitioners report an emotional and physical high lasting up to several hours after casting, others, more subtle effects. Witches speak of "earthing" stray power at the end of a ritual to tie off or finish the energetic "knot," and all agree that another cleansing and the reversal of the initial protection ritual used can be used to ease the return transition to normal consciousness. For example, if the elemental watchtowers are called at the beginning of the spell, expressing gratitude and "releasing" them at the end eases transition. A small amount of food and drink is a time-honored method of celebration and of denoting the return to regular space and consciousness.

Care must be taken to "cut the cord" after every spell, freeing the released energy to do its work without interference. This may be done as a matter of course when the protections are reversed, or with a magickal object such as an athame or wand just before the return to normal consciousness.

Afterward, it becomes simply a question of watching for effects.

PART VIII

CLEANSING (AGAIN)

FAILURE, SUCCESS

Many practitioners advocate cleansing not only at the beginning of a spell but at the end. Again, censing, ablution, "sweeping" the space with wand or besom, etc., are all effective, and it is a matter of the practitioner's personal taste. By that point, the spell is cast, and all that remains is watchfulness.

The most common cause of spell failure is the refusal to prepare the physical, non-magickal ground for success. It is only rarely that a spell *alone* will bring about the desired effect. The practitioner must prepare for success in and on non-magickal terms to give the spell-seed fertile earth for germination. Other common causes of failure or weak effects are the slippage of the raised energy caused by attention to details other than the desired end at the point of climax and power bleed-off caused by brooding upon or speaking inadvisably about the spell after its consummation.

No doubt skeptics or the religiously fearful will scoff and call it mere luck when a practitioner has arranged everything possible in the physical world before turning to magick. There is no answer for such nay-saying other than personal experience and observation. If a matter is important enough for you to bring the Art to bear upon it, there is no reason not to use every tool one has to induce success.

A properly performed spell is powerful; how much more so can it be when every possible condition has been arranged for its success? Chance favors the prepared, and what is magick but putting a thumb upon luck's scales?

Of far more interest and usefulness than brooding upon naysayers is contemplation of the sideways nature of successes. Magick often works with great subtlety, camouflaging itself as chance or accident. For this reason it is highly recommended that records be kept, in order to show patterns and conditions of success—we shall approach that subject in a short while.

First, though, we must speak of silence.

PART IX

MOUTH SHUT, EARS OPEN

KEEPING SILENCE

Practicing silence after a spell's conclusion performs a number of functions. For a new practitioner gaining confidence in their own power and methods, it is a protective cloak. It is difficult enough working in solitude; critical or inadvisable words from the uninitiated may destroy necessary confidence and cause the new practitioner to doubt their work, bleeding away necessary energy. It is also a protection for the experienced or adept practitioner—what the uninitiated don't know about cannot get you burned alive, whether literally or figuratively.

When in doubt about sharing with the uninitiated, do not.

The practice of silence also strengthens a practitioner's mental discipline and provides a slight but very welcome tension when it becomes time to cast another spell, which can be utilized to create or maintain a slight magickal charge for the next round of work.

There are cases where breaking of silence may be advisable or pleasant, for example, when working with a group of practitioners or performing a work with a mass of onlookers in order to harness crowd energies. Much care must be taken with both—even in a group of serious practitioners the risk of stray emotional influences or peccadilloes growing toxic is marked, and effective practitioners are cats much resistant to herding. Harnessing mass crowd energy can lead to deep, unpleasant energy hangovers; performing a mass psychodrama without adequate protections for the individual practitioner's psychic well-being is distinctly *not* recommended for obvious reasons.

All that aside, the quieter a practitioner is about their work, the more chance they have of success *and* of escaping notice. Even in this modern age, those with extraordinary abilities or skills are vulnerable to reprisals from those who fear any sign of greatness.

This does not mean a practitioner shouldn't keep records, however. While laying your intimate works before family, friends, or strangers is not recommended, the keeping of a grimoire most definitely is.

PART X

KEEPING RECORDS

GRIMOIRE GAMES

Grimoire, Book of Shadows, diary—no matter what one calls it, a record of one's magickal practice is invaluable. It is a repository for confidences that can reduce the stress of holding silence while still keeping its more powerful tension, a quick-reference or memory aid, and it provides a sense of proportion and the ability to more easily spot patterns and effects.

Some practitioners invest heavily in beautiful blank books they then do not write in for fear of being messy. The best is often the simplest, an outwardly anonymous notebook a practitioner can carry anywhere without exciting comment or curiosity. Special inks or tools can be purchased or commissioned, as long as the practitioner remembers that *actual use* is the mark of a true grimoire. Illustrations are only as necessary as the personal preference of the practitioner. A cipher may or may not be useful, depending on whether the practice of it interferes with utility.

Noting such things as tides, astronomical or astrological correspondences and events, mood, daily divination, and daily trance practice can help a practitioner spot extremely useful patterns; the practice and discipline of writing down such things indubitably helps in the event of an emergency requiring the quick trigger ritual or ritual consciousness.

Some practitioners use electronic means to keep their grimoires, which is advisable only if useful and secure. In cases of disability, ease of use becomes paramount; whatever helps a practitioner keep regular disciplined records is admissible and even admirable.

Setting aside time—ideally weekly, but more often in practice monthly—to glance through one's grimoire in order to refresh the memory and gain encouragement is highly useful. Knowing the patterns of magickal work that provide one with the greatest results is the entire point of ongoing mastery of the Art.

The deep practice of magick is not easy, therefore, there is no reason to avoid giving oneself all possible advantage.

PART XI

STAY FLEXIBLE

VALUABLE DISCOURAGEMENT

The annals of magick are full of practitioners who fell prey to laziness, drug abuse, verbal incontinence, or discouragement, and full of those who engage in cultural appropriation or outright abuse attempting to gain power via shortcut. Of these various cautionary examples, only discouragement has not been addressed so far. Plenty of successful practitioners have no doubt passed unnoticed and unheralded, their records moldering in peace or destroyed by well-meaning family or friends after their demise.

One suspects they might not mind so much, having achieved their aims while alive.

Discouragement can strike when one's spell effects appear invalid or even actively contradictory. Even a negative effect is still an *effect*, and should be taken as a comforting sign that one's technique is at least providing some results. Altering a spell and further experimenting is the best way to stave off discouragement; keeping oneself busy until desired results appear leaves little time for moping or second-guessing. In magick, as in life, there is no substitute for hard, disciplined work.

Some discouragement is natural and healthy—otherwise, why would we bother aiming for more, for better? Rereading your grimoire will show you progress to combat unhealthy pessimism, and also give you plenty of ideas for further alteration and refinement of your practice to grant better results.

A healthy dose of stubbornness is a great aid, too, and is often a defining feature of a successful practitioner. Care must be taken to not let such a valuable discipline turn into toxic contrariness simply for the sake of it, and also to puncture any ego-bubbles threatening to induce the practitioner to believe their own public relations, so to speak. A tense balance between stubbornness and humility is the best policy, and requires an active balancing rather than a passive sinking into defeatism.

If, no matter the alteration, a spell is not working, lay it aside and focus on other areas and other works for a specific period of time—three months is the general rule. Upon revisiting, the reason for the difficulty will often appear, and is generally a realization of a deep error in the framing of the desire the spell is to bring to fruition. How you state your desires in the initial stage of building a spell is key, and only practice will give you the necessary self-knowledge and experience to choose the best scaffolding as well as the best methods to bring it about.

AFTERWORD

It doesn't matter to the author why you wish to practice magick. Your reasons are your own. The author's aim is to give you the simple, primary tools to do so effectively because the more practitioners there are, the safer the author become hidden in that mass. The satisfaction of giving people tools for their own liberation is considerable, but in the end only an afterthought.

✦

Now it's up to you.

PART XII

APPENDICES

APPENDIX 1: SAMPLE GRIMOIRE ENTRY

Sample Grimoire Spell Entry (as distinct from divination, mood, illustration, research, or other entries)

✦

AIM: What am I hoping to achieve? What simple way can I state my desire?

✦

CORRESPONDENCES: Which details—moon phase, candle color, incense, astrological sign, astronomical event, to name a few—will help me best use the natural forces available and trigger ritual consciousness? How will I acquire the necessary supplies?

✦

INITIAL DIVINATION: What roadblocks can I see? What warnings am I receiving? What can I do to avoid problems or ill effects?

✴

STRUCTURE: What cleansing and protection rituals will I use? How will I raise the energy? What will I chant, if required, and what will I do if an unexpected event breaks my concentration?

✴

DIVINATION PROPER: What effects are likely?

✴

PERFORMED: Date and time performed.

✴

IMMEDIATE EFFECT(s): If any.

✴

CHECK INS: How often will I check for results?

✴

OTHER EFFECT(s): If any.

✴

WHAT WAS LEARNED: Was the spell effective? Were there warnings I didn't see?

APPENDIX 2: SAMPLE SPELLBUILDING WORKSHEET

What is my aim?

✪

What forces/correspondences can I channel to help achieve it?

✪

What have I physically done to prepare the ground? Could I do more?

✪

What is the best structure for this spell? What is the best fuel for it?

✪

What hazards can I see ahead of time, and how can they be addressed?

✪

How do I intend to work outside of ritual/magickal space to achieve my aim?

How many times should I repeat this spell for maximum results?

What physical objects will I need for casting?

What will I consider a success? Incomplete success? Failure?

ABOUT THE AUTHOR

El Morningstar is a pseudonym, for obvious reasons.

www.ingramcontent.com/pod-product-compliance
Lightning Source LLC
Chambersburg PA
CBHW071245020426
42333CB00015B/1630